Dip!

Text © Nuala King 2025
Illustrations © Essi Kimpimäki 2025

Published in 2025 by Welbeck
An Imprint of HEADLINE PUBLISHING GROUP LIMITED

1

Cataloguing in Publication Data is available from the British Library

ISBN 9781035424276

Printed in China

Headline's policy is to use papers that are natural, renewable and recyclable
products and made from wood grown in well-managed forests and other controlled
sources. The logging and manufacturing processes are expected to conform to the
environmental regulations of the country of origin.

Editor: Emma Hanson
Design: James Empringham
Production: Arlene Lestrade

HEADLINE PUBLISHING GROUP LIMITED
An Hachette UK Company
Carmelite House
50 Victoria Embankment
London EC4Y 0DZ

The authorized representative in the EEA is Hachette Ireland,
8 Castlecourt Centre, Dublin 15, D15 XTP3, Ireland (email: info@hbgi.ie)

www.headline.co.uk
www.hachette.co.uk

Dip!

**75 speedy, simple, savoury
and sweet dip recipes**

NUALA KING

WITH ILLUSTRATIONS BY
ESSI KIMPIMÄKI

WELBECK

CONTENTS

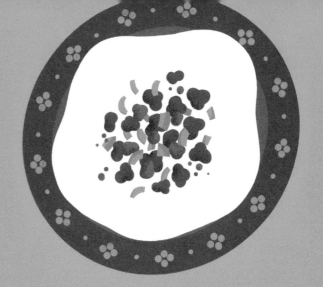

INTRO

For me, dips are an essential part of hosting. At a dinner party, putting some crisps and a dip on the table will afford you that extra 20 minutes to cook that you didn't anticipate needing. When hosting people for drinks, a big spread of dips with crudités, bread and crackers is a total crowd-pleaser. Perfect for taking to a picnic, BBQ or potluck, dips are always a useful thing to have in your fridge. They are quick to make, often use simple, inexpensive ingredients, and can cater to all likes and dislikes, dietary requirements and seasons.

This book is full of versatile, speedy and, most importantly, simple dip recipes. With 75 recipes divided into six chapters, you'll find a dip for every occasion. If making a few, try picking a recipe from each chapter to ensure a vibrant and varied spread.

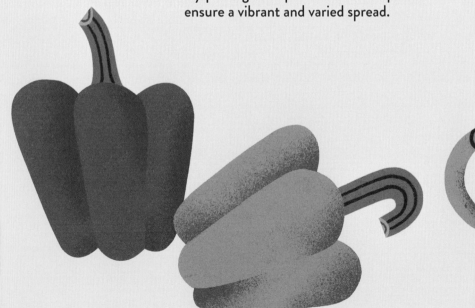

A FEW NOTES ON THE RECIPES:

Each recipe serves 4–6 as a stand-alone dish, but this is a guideline only; they will serve more or fewer people depending on hunger and how they are served.

I call for flaky sea salt in all recipes as it's what I use at home, but use fine sea salt for seasoning if you prefer. Always use flaky salt to finish if you can.

All the recipes can be adjusted to suit your favourite flavours or what you can find in your kitchen: use yoghurt in place of sour cream, chickpeas in place of butter beans, parsley in place of basil, onions in place of shallots – you get the idea. The most important thing is to taste as you go along.

Happy dipping!

CREAMY DIPS

This cooling, garlicky yoghurt is delicious eaten with bread or crudités, but if I have it in my fridge I find myself adding a dollop of it to almost everything. Add to sandwiches, serve with grilled meat or vegetables, use it in a potato salad, or eat it with a spoon.

TZATZIKI

½ cucumber

300g (10½oz) thick Greek yoghurt

1 garlic clove, minced

1 tablespoon red wine vinegar

1 tablespoon extra virgin olive oil, plus extra to serve

10g (¼oz) mint leaves, finely chopped

10g (¼oz) dill, finely chopped

Flaky sea salt

Coarsely grate the cucumber then place in a sieve set over a bowl. Sprinkle with salt and leave for 10–15 minutes to allow some of the liquid to drain.

Meanwhile, add the yoghurt, garlic, vinegar, olive oil and herbs to a large mixing bowl, along with a generous pinch of salt, and stir well to combine. Add the cucumber and mix again. Taste to check the seasoning, adding more salt if desired. Serve with an extra drizzle of olive oil.

Making labneh is amazing – your natural yoghurt can transform into this thick, cream-cheese-like texture with little to no effort. Your desired thickness will inform how long you leave it to hang out in the fridge, but in this instance I think it's best still slightly loose, to enable good dipping. Here are some ideas for variations, but get creative with whatever you've got. I like to eat these with grilled bread.

LABNEH

¼ teaspoon fine sea salt

450g (1lb) natural yoghurt

Extra virgin olive oil, to serve

Line a sieve with a cheesecloth or a J-cloth and set over a mixing bowl. Mix the salt into the yoghurt, then spoon into the lined sieve. Tie up the corners, then transfer to the fridge for 2–3 hours, or until it reaches your desired consistency. You can place something heavy on top, like a can of food, to encourage the liquid to drain.

Remove from the fridge and spread on to a plate. Drizzle with extra virgin olive oil to serve.

LABNEH WITH BROWNED BUTTER

30g (1oz) salted butter, cubed

Juice of ½ lemon

1 quantity of labneh (see opposite)

Add the cubed butter to a sauté pan and set over a medium heat. Cook for 5–10 minutes, keeping a close eye on it when it starts to foam so it doesn't burn. It's ready when it smells nutty and you can see golden flecks at the bottom of the pan. Remove from the heat and add a squeeze of lemon juice, adding more if desired.

To serve, spread the labneh on to a plate and pour the browned butter over the top.

LABNEH WITH CURRIED ONIONS

1 tablespoon extra virgin olive oil

10g (¼oz) unsalted butter

1 onion, thinly sliced

½ tablespoon medium curry powder

Juice of ½ lemon or lime

1 quantity of labneh (see page 12)

Flaky sea salt

Add the olive oil and butter to a frying pan and set over a medium-low heat. Add the onion along with a pinch of salt and cook gently for 10–15 minutes until softened. Add the curry powder and cook for a final 2–3 minutes. Remove from the heat and squeeze in the lemon or lime juice.

Spread the labneh on to a plate and spoon the curried onions over the top, along with any residual fat from the pan.

This comes together in five minutes and is a great addition to any mezze platter or meal. Dip your veggies in, serve at a BBQ with meat, or simply eat with crisps.

TAHINI YOGHURT

200g (7oz) thick Greek yoghurt

50g (2oz) tahini

1 garlic clove, minced

Juice of ½–1 lemon, to taste

1 tablespoon extra virgin olive oil

Flaky sea salt

Sumac, to serve

Add the yoghurt, tahini, garlic, juice of ½ lemon and olive oil to a bowl along with a generous pinch of salt. Whisk together until smooth and combined. If it is too thick, add a splash of cold water to loosen. Taste, adding more lemon juice or salt if needed. Serve with a sprinkle of sumac.

A riff on baba ganoush, but with the addition of yoghurt and nuts. It's smoky, tangy and quick to come together.

SMOKY AUBERGINE AND YOGHURT DIP

1 aubergine

100g (3½oz) thick Greek yoghurt

1 garlic clove, minced

2 tablespoons tahini

Juice of 1 lemon

30g (1oz) walnuts, toasted and chopped

½ small bunch of parsley, leaves finely chopped

1 tablespoon extra virgin olive oil, plus extra to serve

Flaky sea salt

Pierce the aubergine all over with a fork. Char it over a flame for 10–15 minutes, turning often, until completely blackened and collapsing; you can do this under the grill if you don't have a gas hob. Transfer to a colander in the sink, cut into it lengthways, then leave to cool and drain a bit.

Once cooled, peel away most of the charred aubergine skin and remove the stem. Place the flesh in a bowl and break up with a fork. Add the yoghurt, garlic, tahini, lemon juice, walnuts, parsley, olive oil and a good pinch of salt. Stir well to combine, then taste and add more salt if needed.

I love this dip – a chic take on sour cream and chive with the delicious addition of caramelized onions. Don't rush cooking them; I promise it's worth it. Eat with your favourite crisps – I like something crinkly here.

FRENCH ONION DIP

1 tablespoon extra virgin olive oil

20g (¾oz) unsalted butter

1 onion, finely chopped

1 garlic clove, minced

3 sprigs of thyme, leaves picked

150g (5oz) sour cream

50g (2oz) mayonnaise

50g (2oz) cream cheese

Juice of ½ lemon

½ shallot, finely chopped

Flaky sea salt and ground black pepper

10g (¾oz) chives, finely chopped, to serve

Add the olive oil and butter to a frying pan and set over a medium heat. Add the onion and cook for 25–30 minutes, until caramelized, adding the garlic and thyme for the final 2 minutes. Set aside to cool.

Once cooled, add to a mixing bowl along with the sour cream, mayonnaise, cream cheese, lemon juice and shallot. Stir to combine, then season to taste with salt and pepper and serve scattered with the chives.

A classic for very good reason. Once you realize how easy it is to make at home, you'll be making this for every dip spread.

SOUR CREAM AND CHIVE

150g (5oz) sour cream

75g (2½oz) mayonnaise

½ shallot, finely chopped

Juice of ½ lemon

10g (¼oz) chives, finely chopped

Flaky sea salt

Mix the sour cream, mayonnaise, shallot, lemon juice and most of the chives in a bowl, then season to taste with salt. Serve with the remaining chives sprinkled on top.

This kimchi dip originating from Hawaii was first introduced to me by food writer Esther Clark and it is so so good. I've added crispy chilli oil here for an extra kick, but put your own spin on this. Start with kimchi, cream cheese and sour cream and see where you end up!

KIMCHI DIP

100g (3½oz) drained kimchi, chopped

165g (6oz) cream cheese

100g (3½oz) sour cream

2 spring onions, thinly sliced

½ tablespoon crispy chilli oil

1 teaspoon light soy sauce

A few splashes of Worcestershire sauce

Juice of ½ lemon

Black sesame seeds, toasted, to serve

Add the chopped kimchi, cream cheese, sour cream, spring onions, crispy chilli oil and soy sauce to a bowl and mix very well until combined. Add the Worcestershire sauce and lemon juice and stir again. Serve with black sesame seeds scattered over the top.

Serve with dough balls, focaccia, warm ciabatta, pizza crusts... the options are endless.

GARLIC BUTTER

100g (3½oz) salted butter, softened

10g (¼oz) parsley, leaves picked and finely chopped

1–2 garlic cloves, minced

1 tablespoon extra virgin olive oil

Flaky sea salt

In a small bowl, combine the softened butter with the parsley, 1 clove of minced garlic and the olive oil. Season to taste with salt, adding more garlic too if you want it to be punchier!

This transforms a block of tofu into something so creamy and perfect for dipping. Topped with the lemony, fried courgettes, it's a great dish to have at a BBQ.

WHIPPED TOFU WITH FRAZZLED COURGETTES

5 tablespoons extra virgin olive oil, plus extra to serve

1 courgette, thinly sliced into rounds

Grated zest and juice of 1 lemon

½ small bunch of mint, leaves shredded

300g (10½oz) block of firm tofu (in water), drained

2 tablespoons tahini

1 garlic clove, minced

Flaky sea salt and ground black pepper

Drizzle of honey, to serve

Sprinkle of chilli flakes, to serve

Set a frying pan over a medium heat and add 2 tablespoons of the olive oil. Once hot, add the sliced courgettes and fry for 6–8 minutes until golden. Do this in batches if necessary so that you keep the courgettes in one layer. Once cooked, transfer to a bowl and add the lemon zest and half the lemon juice, and the shredded mint.

Add the tofu to a food processor and blitz until smooth. Add the remaining 3 tablespoons of olive oil, the remaining lemon juice, the tahini, the garlic and a generous pinch each of salt and pepper, then blitz again. Taste, adjusting the seasoning as necessary.

Spread the whipped tofu over a serving dish and top with the courgettes. Finish with a drizzle of honey, a sprinkle of chilli flakes and an extra bit of olive oil.

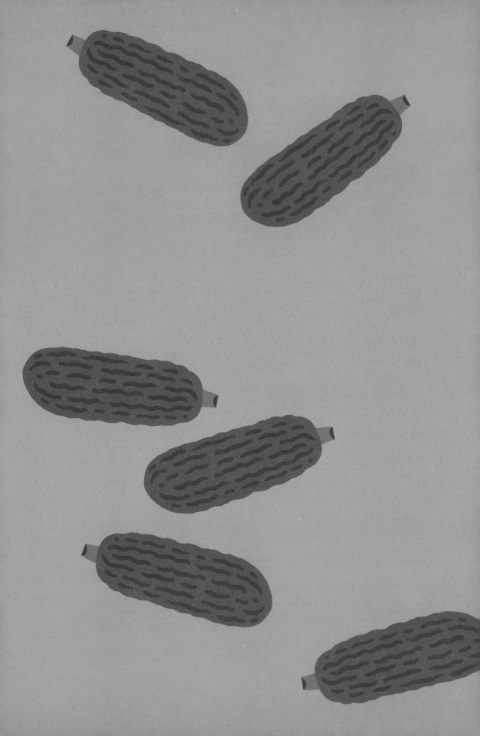

I love anything pickled, and this dip is no exception. Do experiment with other pickled veg – carrots would be delicious. For a more intense pickle flavour, add a little of the brine from one of the pickle jars and serve alongside dill or pickled onion flavoured crisps.

PICKLE DIP

80g (3oz) pickled gherkins or cornichons, finely chopped

50g (2oz) sauerkraut, finely chopped

30g (1oz) pickled jalapeños, finely chopped

200g (7oz) sour cream

80g (3oz) mayonnaise

1 tablespoon wholegrain mustard

Juice of ½–1 lemon, to taste

Small bunch of dill, finely chopped

Flaky sea salt

Mix the gherkins, sauerkraut, jalapeños, sour cream, mayonnaise, mustard, the juice of ½ lemon and the dill in a bowl until well combined. Season to taste with salt, and more lemon juice if needed.

What's better than eating crisps and aioli on holiday after a day in the sun? Not much. This simple, cheat's version is absolutely not traditional, but hits the spot and requires very little hands-on time. Dip your crisps, veg or bread in this, but you'll want some leftovers for a sandwich or potato salad too.

CHEAT'S AIOLI

1 whole head of garlic, plus an extra clove

1 teaspoon extra virgin olive oil

120g (4oz) mayonnaise

50g (2oz) thick Greek yoghurt

Flaky sea salt and ground black pepper

Preheat the oven to 180°C/160°C fan (350°F) Gas 4.

Place the garlic bulb on a small sheet of foil. Peel away the outer papery layers, then cut off the very top to reveal the cloves. Drizzle the olive oil over the top, then scrunch the foil to seal. Transfer to the oven to roast for 30–40 minutes, then set aside to cool down.

Squeeze the cooled garlic out into a bowl and mash with a fork. Add the mayonnaise, yoghurt, a generous amount of black pepper and some salt to taste. If you want a more intense garlic flavour, grate in half the extra garlic clove and taste again. Add the other half if you want it to be even punchier, but the flavour will intensify with time, so proceed with caution!

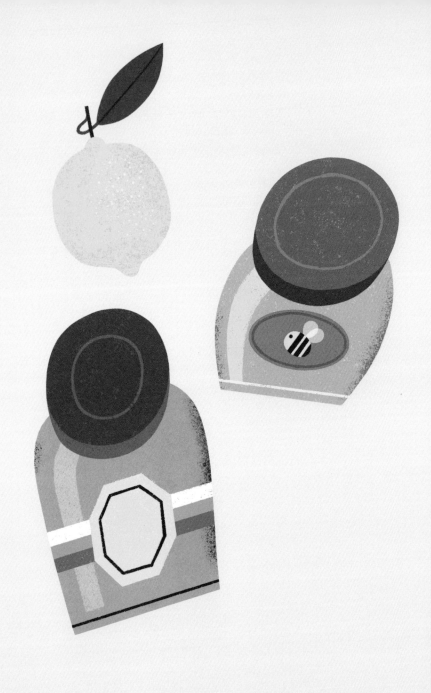

This is my favourite sauce for any kind of fried chicken, but dip anything in this and it'll be delicious.

HONEY MUSTARD

50g (2oz) mayonnaise

50g (2oz) thick Greek yoghurt or sour cream

2 tablespoons American mustard

1 tablespoon Dijon mustard

½ tablespoon honey, or more to taste

Juice of ½ lemon

Sea salt and ground black pepper

Mix the mayonnaise, yoghurt or sour cream, mustards, honey and lemon juice together in a bowl until combined. Season to taste with salt and pepper, adding more honey, mustard or lemon if desired.

I love a bagel, I love cream cheese and I love everything bagel seasoning. This dip is an ode to these flavours – definitely serve this with bagel chips if you can find them, or make your own!

EVERYTHING BAGEL DIP

100g (3½oz) cream cheese

100g (3½oz) sour cream

2 spring onions, thinly sliced

1 teaspoon dried minced garlic

1 teaspoon onion granules

1 teaspoon black sesame seeds

1 teaspoon white sesame seeds

Juice of ½–1 lemon, to taste

Flaky sea salt

In a bowl, mix the cream cheese, sour cream, spring onions, dried garlic, onion granules, black and white sesame seeds and the juice of ½ lemon. Season to taste with salt and add some more lemon juice if needed.

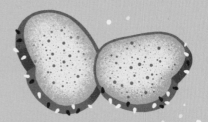

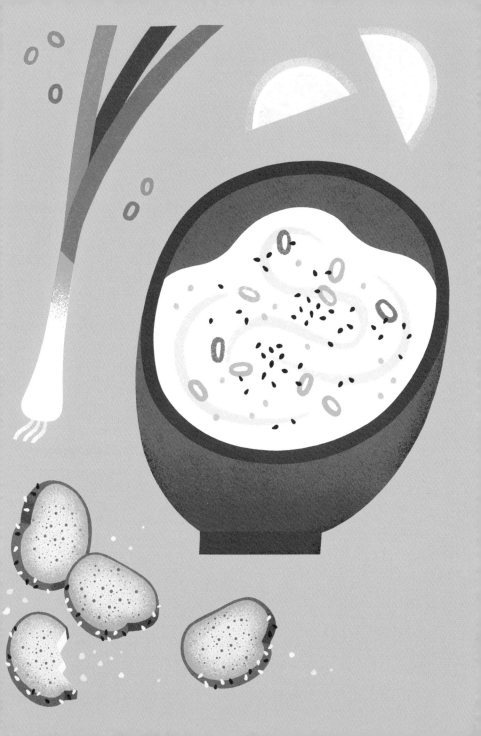

Does this recipe need an introduction? A Caesar salad is unrivalled and this is a great dip to have in your rotation. Dip romaine leaves (put them in iced water first to get extra crunchy!), roasted tenderstem broccoli, grilled chicken, or just crisps. It's delicious!

CAESAR DIP

2 anchovies in oil (optional)

150g (5oz) thick Greek yoghurt

50g (2oz) mayonnaise

1 garlic clove, minced

1 tablespoon Dijon mustard

Juice of ½ lemon

50g (2oz) Parmesan, finely grated

A few good splashes of Worcestershire sauce

30 grinds of black pepper

Flaky sea salt (optional)

If using anchovies, add these first into a mixing bowl and use a fork to mash them as much as you can. Add the yoghurt, mayonnaise, garlic, mustard, lemon juice, Parmesan, Worcestershire sauce and pepper and stir to combine. Taste, adding salt and more pepper if needed.

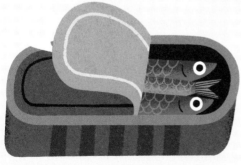

While this is most traditionally paired with chicken, I love serving it as a dip instead. It's great for dipping fries into but also a perfect option to serve with crunchy vegetables or crisps.

CORONATION DIP

200g (7oz) thick Greek yoghurt

100g (3½oz) mayonnaise

3 tablespoons mango chutney

1 tablespoon mild curry powder

Handful of sultanas

Flaky sea salt

Toasted flaked almonds, to serve

Mix the yoghurt, mayonnaise, mango chutney, curry powder and sultanas together in a bowl, then season to taste with salt. Sprinkle over the flaked almonds to serve.

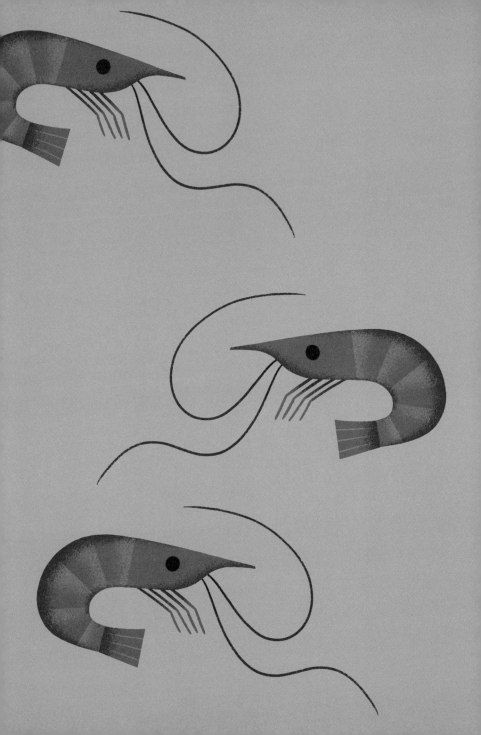

This retro dip is, of course, delicious served with prawns.

MARIE ROSE

80g (3oz) mayonnaise

40g (1½oz) ketchup

A few splashes of Worcestershire sauce

A few splashes of Tabasco

Juice of up to ½ lemon

Flaky sea salt and ground black pepper

Mix the mayonnaise and ketchup together in a bowl. Add a couple of splashes of Worcestershire sauce and Tabasco, a squeeze of lemon juice, and some salt and pepper. Mix together and taste, adding more Worcestershire sauce, Tabasco, lemon juice and seasoning as needed.

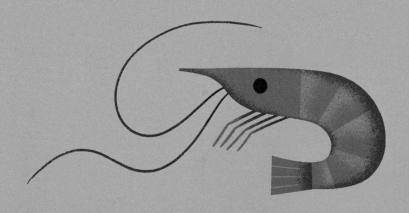

BLUE CHEESE *46*

SPINACH AND ARTICHOKE DIP *48*

WHIPPED FETA *50*

BEETROOT WHIPPED FETA *52*

WHIPPED RICOTTA WITH MARINATED PEPPERS *54*

WHIPPED COTTAGE CHEESE WITH MARINATED TOMATOES *56*

BAKED CAMEMBERT WITH JALAPEÑO RELISH *58*

PIMENTO CHEESE DIP *60*

BAKED GOAT'S CHEESE WITH BLUEBERRIES *62*

BEER CHEESE *64*

QUESO DIP *66*

PECORINO AND SUN-DRIED TOMATO DIP *68*

CHEAT'S STRACCIATELLA WITH PISTACHIO PESTO *70*

CHEESY DIPS

This rich, tangy dip is great served with something spicy – of course, chicken wings are a classic combination, but make spicy tofu or cauliflower bites for a meat-free option. It's also delicious with raw vegetables, and any leftovers are delicious used in a salad.

BLUE CHEESE

200g (7oz) sour cream

100g (3½oz) mayonnaise

120g (4oz) blue cheese, crumbled

2 spring onions, finely chopped

Juice of 1 lemon

A few splashes of Worcestershire sauce

Up to 1 tablespoon apple cider vinegar or white wine vinegar (optional)

10g (¼oz) chives, finely chopped, to serve

Mix the sour cream, mayonnaise, blue cheese, spring onions, lemon juice and Worcestershire sauce together in a bowl. Taste, adding vinegar if it needs more acidity. Serve with the chives scattered on top.

You can go two ways with this dip: bake it in the oven for a bubbling, cheesy dip, or serve it cold without the mozzarella for a fresher version. Sub in the sour cream for Greek yoghurt if you like.

SPINACH AND ARTICHOKE DIP

200g (7oz) baby spinach leaves

1 tablespoon extra virgin olive oil

1 x 400g (14oz) can of artichoke hearts or jarred artichoke hearts in oil, drained and roughly chopped

1 garlic clove, minced

½ teaspoon chilli flakes

100g (3½oz) cream cheese

100g (3½oz) sour cream

40g (1½oz) Parmesan or pecorino, grated

100g (3½oz) low moisture mozzarella, grated or torn (optional, if serving hot)

Juice of ½–1 lemon, to taste

Flaky sea salt and ground black pepper

If serving hot, preheat the oven to 200°C/180°C fan (400°F) Gas 6.

Boil the kettle and add the spinach to a colander placed in the sink. Pour the freshly boiled water over the spinach then run it under the cold tap until cool enough to handle. Squeeze out as much liquid as possible, then finely chop.

Heat the olive oil in an ovenproof frying pan then add the artichokes. Cook over a medium-high heat for 3–5 minutes until lightly golden. Add the garlic and chilli flakes and cook for a further 2 minutes, then add the chopped spinach, cream cheese, sour cream, Parmesan or pecorino and half the mozzarella, if using. Mix until fully combined then squeeze in the juice of ½ lemon. Taste, adding more lemon juice if needed, along with salt and pepper to taste.

If serving cold, set aside to cool, then transfer to the fridge. If serving hot, scatter over the remaining mozzarella and transfer to the oven for 15–20 minutes until golden and bubbling.

This dish is delicious as it is, but make sure to try serving it with different toppings too. Try marinated vegetables, jammy figs, or different herbs and spices.

WHIPPED FETA

200g (7oz) feta

100g (3½oz) thick Greek yoghurt

Grated zest of 1 lemon and juice of ½

Honey, to serve

Extra virgin olive oil, to serve

½ teaspoon Aleppo chilli flakes (pul biber), to serve

Add the feta to a food processor and blitz until broken down. Add the yoghurt, lemon zest and juice, and blitz again until smooth. Serve the whipped feta drizzled with honey, olive oil and the chilli flakes.

This dip is totally delicious, but what really makes it stand out is its vibrant colour. Plus, it's a great way to sneak some extra vegetables in.

BEETROOT WHIPPED FETA

200g (7oz) feta

100g (3½oz) cooked beetroot

Grated zest of 1 lemon

1 tablespoon extra virgin olive oil, plus extra to serve

2 tablespoons mixed seeds, to serve

Small handful of dill, roughly chopped, to serve

Add the feta to a food processor and blitz until broken down. Add the beetroot, lemon zest and olive oil and blitz again until smooth. Serve with the mixed seeds and dill scattered over the top and an extra drizzle of olive oil.

Lemony ricotta and marinated peppers – a match made in heaven. Leaving the peppers to hang out in the oil and vinegar will make this especially delicious, and means you're one step ahead when it comes to serving!

WHIPPED RICOTTA WITH MARINATED PEPPERS

20g (¾oz) blanched almonds

2 roasted red peppers from a jar, thinly sliced

2 tablespoons extra virgin olive oil

1 tablespoon good-quality sherry vinegar

½ small bunch of fresh oregano, leaves picked

250g (9oz) ricotta

50g (2oz) Parmesan, finely grated

Zest of ½ lemon

Flaky sea salt and ground black pepper

Preheat the oven to 180°C/160°C fan (350°F) Gas 4. Add the almonds to a baking tray then transfer to the oven to toast for 8–10 minutes until golden

Add the sliced red peppers, olive oil, vinegar and oregano to a bowl and toss, then season with salt.

In a separate bowl, whisk the ricotta and Parmesan together until smooth. Add the lemon zest and mix again, seasoning to taste with salt and pepper.

When you are ready to serve, add the nuts to the peppers and stir to combine. Spread the ricotta mixture over your serving dish and spoon the peppers into the centre. Serve with an extra grinding of black pepper.

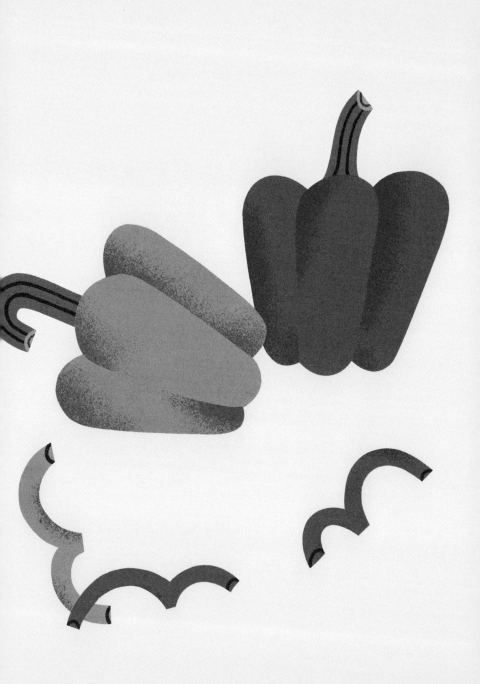

When you blitz cottage cheese, it transforms into a delicious creamy and light mixture. Served with tomatoes, this is a great addition to your summer table.

WHIPPED COTTAGE CHEESE WITH MARINATED TOMATOES

150g (5oz) cherry tomatoes, quartered

2 tablespoons extra virgin olive oil, plus extra to serve

1 tablespoon red wine vinegar or sherry vinegar

½ teaspoon honey

1 garlic clove, minced

Small handful of basil leaves

300g (10½oz) cottage cheese

Flaky sea salt and ground black pepper

Toss the quartered cherry tomatoes in a bowl with the olive oil, vinegar, honey, garlic and basil leaves. Season with salt and set aside to marinate.

Meanwhile, add the cottage cheese to a food processor and blitz until smooth. Season to taste with plenty of salt and black pepper.

Serve the whipped cottage cheese spread over a serving dish, with the marinated tomatoes and their juices spooned into the centre. Finish with more black pepper and an extra drizzle of olive oil.

As much as I love baked, melty cheese, my favourite part of this dip is the relish. It's sweet and spicy, perfect to pair with the richness of the Camembert. Plus, you'll definitely have a little relish left over, so stick it in a sandwich or toastie and enjoy again.

BAKED CAMEMBERT WITH JALAPEÑO RELISH

1 x 250g (9oz) Camembert cheese

Extra virgin olive oil, to drizzle

FOR THE JALAPEÑO RELISH

50g (2oz) pickled jalapeños, finely chopped

80g (3oz) pickled gherkins, finely chopped

1 small green apple, peeled, cored and finely diced

1 shallot, finely chopped

1 garlic clove, minced

75g (2½oz) honey, plus extra to serve

2 tablespoons apple cider vinegar

1 tablespoon wholegrain mustard

½ small bunch of dill, finely chopped

Start by making the jalapeño relish. Add the jalapeños, gherkins, apple, shallot, garlic, honey, vinegar and mustard to a small saucepan and set over a medium heat. Bring to the boil, then turn down and simmer for 10–15 minutes. Remove from the heat, stir through the dill and set aside to cool completely.

Preheat the oven to 200°C/180°C fan (400°F) Gas 6. Remove any plastic wrapping from the Camembert, then place it back in the bottom half of its box. Score a criss-cross pattern in the top of the cheese, then drizzle with a little olive oil. Transfer to the oven and bake for about 20 minutes, until gooey and bubbling.

Remove from the oven and place on a plate, then spoon some of the jalapeño relish over the top. Tuck in, making sure to get plenty of cheese and relish when you dunk.

This dip is a big deal in the US yet less known elsewhere, but it's a great one to add to your repertoire. Serve with chicory leaves, crackers or bread, and serve leftovers sandwiched between slices of soft white bread.

PIMENTO CHEESE DIP

150g (5oz) cream cheese

50g (2oz) mature Cheddar, grated

100g (3½oz) roasted red peppers from a jar, finely chopped (use pimento peppers if you can)

25g (1oz) mayonnaise

½ teaspoon cayenne pepper, plus extra to serve

Juice of ½–1 lemon, to taste

1 garlic clove, minced

1 fresh jalapeño, red or green chilli, finely chopped

Flaky sea salt and ground black pepper

Add the cream cheese, Cheddar, red peppers, mayonnaise, cayenne pepper, juice of ½ lemon, garlic and jalapeño to a bowl and mix until well combined. Season to taste with salt and pepper, adding more lemon juice if needed. Serve with an extra bit of cayenne on top.

I love making this as part of a big summer lunch. I've opted for using a log of goat's cheese, so make sure to cut into it when you serve for easier dipping! Try switching the blueberries for blackberries, if you prefer.

BAKED GOAT'S CHEESE WITH BLUEBERRIES

1 x 150g (5oz) goat's cheese log

2 tablespoons extra virgin olive oil

1 tablespoon honey

1 sprig of rosemary, leaves finely chopped

100g (3½oz) blueberries (optional)

Flaky sea salt

Preheat the oven to 200°C/180°C fan (400°F) Gas 6.

Place the goat's cheese in an ovenproof dish and drizzle over 1 tablespoon of the olive oil and the honey, sprinkling the rosemary and a little salt on top. Arrange the blueberries around the cheese then drizzle them with the remaining tablespoon of olive oil.

Transfer to the oven to bake for 15–20 minutes, until the blueberries are starting to break down and the cheese is lightly golden. Remove from the oven and use a fork to gently squash the blueberries, releasing some of their juices. Serve immediately.

This pub-style cheese dip is comforting and indulgent. Most often you'll find it served with pretzels (the bread kind), but serve with whatever bread you fancy.

BEER CHEESE

30g (1oz) butter

30g (1oz) plain flour

180ml (6fl oz) whole milk

120ml (4fl oz) beer (I like an IPA)

1 tablespoon Dijon mustard

A few splashes of Worcestershire sauce

½ teaspoon smoked paprika

½ teaspoon garlic granules

½ teaspoon onion granules

100g (3½oz) extra mature Cheddar, grated

Flaky sea salt and ground black pepper

Small bunch of chives, finely chopped, to serve

Start by making a roux. Melt the butter in a medium saucepan over a medium heat, then add the flour and stir continuously, using a balloon whisk, until a paste forms. Cook for 2 minutes, then gradually add the beer, whisking constantly. Next, slowly pour in the milk, whisking all the time. Cook for 5–10 minutes until thickened, then add the mustard, Worcestershire sauce, smoked paprika and garlic and onion granules, and whisk well until combined.

Finally, add the grated cheese and whisk again until melted and totally smooth. Taste, adding more salt, pepper or Worcestershire sauce as needed.

Scatter with the chives to serve.

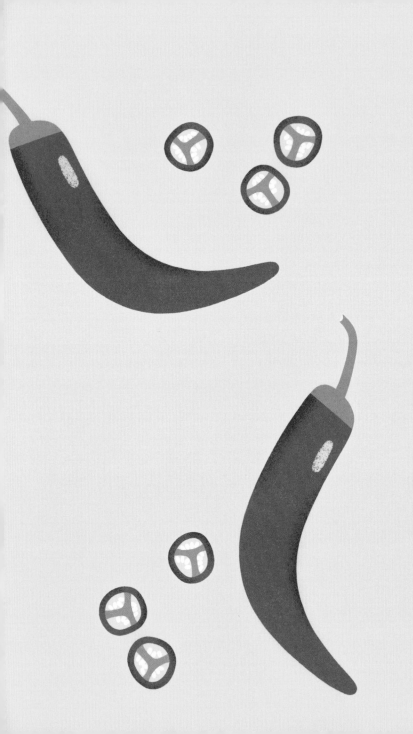

This popular dip inspired by Mexican and Tex-Mex cooking is utterly addictive, and I always eat so much that by the time my main arrives, I'm full. The pickled jalapeños cut through the cheese but I like to serve this with salsa and guac too in order to keep things fresh!

QUESO DIP

½ onion, finely chopped

1 tablespoon extra virgin olive oil

10g (¼oz) unsalted butter

1 teaspoon cayenne pepper

25g (1oz) pickled jalapeños, finely chopped, plus ½ tablespoon of their pickling juice

200ml (7fl oz) evaporated milk

100g (3½oz) American cheese, finely chopped

100g (3½oz) mature Cheddar, grated

50g (2oz) sour cream

Flaky sea salt

Add the onion to a saucepan along with the olive oil, butter and a pinch of salt. Fry for 10 minutes over a medium heat until softened but not taking on any colour, then add the cayenne and chopped jalapeños and cook for 2 minutes longer.

Tip in the evaporated milk along with the jalapeño juice and cheeses. Lower the heat and whisk until thickened and smooth, and the cheese is completely melted, about 8–10 minutes.

Remove from the heat and stir through the sour cream, adding extra salt if needed.

I love pecorino and it goes so well with the basil and sun-dried tomatoes in this dip. I like to scoop this one up with salty, crinkle-cut crisps, but you can dip crunchy or grilled vegetables too. Leftovers would be delicious to dress a pasta or potato salad, or used in a sandwich.

PECORINO AND SUN-DRIED TOMATO DIP

100g (3½oz) sour cream

100g (3½oz) mayonnaise

1–2 tablespoons sun-dried tomato pesto

1 garlic clove, minced

100g (3½oz) pecorino, finely grated

Juice of 1 lemon

Small handful of basil leaves, roughly chopped

Flaky sea salt and ground black pepper

15g (½oz) pine nuts, toasted, to serve

Mix the sour cream, mayonnaise, pesto, garlic, pecorino, lemon juice and basil together in a bowl. Season to taste with salt and pepper, then scatter over the pine nuts to serve.

This dip creates something like the inside of a burrata ball. It's SO easy to make at home and is a great base for many dishes. I've served it here with a quick pesto, but you could serve it with tomatoes, stone fruits, figs, cured meats, or simply olive oil.

CHEAT'S STRACCIATELLA WITH PISTACHIO PESTO

2 x 125g (4oz) balls of mozzarella, torn

125g (4oz) crème fraîche

40g (1½oz) shelled pistachios

60g (2oz) basil leaves

1 garlic clove, minced

30g (1oz) Parmesan, finely grated

100ml (3½fl oz) extra virgin olive oil, plus extra to serve

Juice of ½ lemon

Flaky sea salt and ground black pepper

To make the stracciatella, mix the mozzarella and crème fraîche together in a bowl with a little salt. Transfer to the fridge for an hour.

In the meantime, make the pesto. Add the pistachios, basil, garlic, Parmesan and olive oil to a food processor and blitz until you reach your desired consistency. Season to taste with salt and pepper.

Remove the stracciatella from the fridge and spread over the base of your serving dish. Drizzle the pesto on top, finishing with an extra drizzle of olive oil.

NOTE

This recipe will make more pesto than you'll need, so store it in a sterilized jar topped with an extra drizzle of oil to keep it fresh and green. Use it for pasta, in sandwiches, or simply serve alongside roast chicken or vegetables.

BEAN-BASED DIPS

Once you start to make hummus at home, you won't go back to the shop-bought kind. It's quick, so simple and you can have lots of fun experimenting with different flavours. There are many variations of this Middle-Eastern dip, each with different proportions of the core ingredients. This ratio is my preference, but feel free to add more or less tahini, garlic, lemon juice, or olive oil to suit your taste.

PICKLED JALAPEÑO HUMMUS

240g (8½oz) drained chickpeas, liquid reserved

3 tablespoons tahini

50g (2oz) pickled jalapeños

2 tablespoons extra virgin olive oil

Flaky sea salt

Add the chickpeas to a food processor along with a little of their liquid and blitz until broken down. Add the tahini, jalapeños, olive oil and a good pinch of flaky salt and blitz again until smooth. Taste to check the seasoning, adding more salt if needed. If the hummus is too thick, add a cube of ice or a tablespoon of very cold water and blitz until you reach your desired consistency.

NOTE
I prefer to use jarred beans where possible as they result in a much smoother hummus when blitzed right away, as well as being so delicious. If using canned beans, you can opt for warming them in their liquid over a gentle heat for 15–20 minutes to soften them before blending. Remember to persevere with your blender, too – keep going until you're happy with the texture.

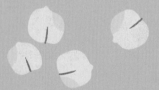

RED PEPPER HUMMUS

240g (8½oz) drained chickpeas, liquid reserved

3 tablespoons tahini

100g (3½oz) roasted red peppers from a jar

Juice of ½–1 lemon, to taste

2 tablespoons extra virgin olive oil

½ teaspoon chilli flakes (optional)

Flaky sea salt

Add the chickpeas to a food processor along with a little of their liquid and blitz until broken down. Add the tahini, red peppers, the juice of ½ lemon, the olive oil, a good pinch of salt and the chilli flakes, if using. Blitz until smooth, then taste to check the seasoning, adding more salt or lemon juice as needed. If the hummus is too thick, add a cube of ice or a tablespoon of very cold water and blitz until you reach your desired consistency.

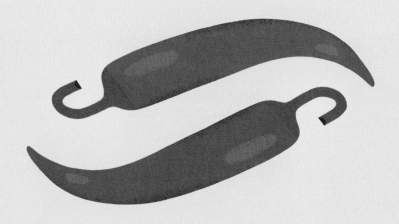

CLASSIC HUMMUS

240g (8½oz) drained chickpeas, liquid reserved

3 tablespoons tahini

Juice of ½–1 lemon, to taste

1–2 garlic cloves, to taste, minced

2 tablespoons extra virgin olive oil, plus extra to serve

Flaky sea salt

Add the chickpeas to a food processor along with a little of their liquid and blitz until broken down. Add the tahini, the juice of ½ lemon, the garlic, olive oil and a good pinch of salt and blitz again until smooth. Taste to check the seasoning, adding more salt, lemon juice and garlic as needed. Blitz again, then taste to check the seasoning once more. If the hummus needs loosening, add an ice cube or a tablespoon of very cold water and blitz again, repeating until you reach your desired consistency.

Serve with an extra drizzle of olive oil.

This crispy chorizo-topped hummus is packed with flavour and so satisfying to eat because of the contrasting textures. Make the hummus ahead of time and fry the chorizo just before serving for an impressive and crowd-pleasing dish.

CHORIZO HUMMUS

240g (8½oz) drained chickpeas, liquid reserved

3 tablespoons tahini

Juice of ½–1 lemon, to taste

1–2 garlic cloves, to taste, minced

2 tablespoons extra virgin olive oil

1 teaspoon smoked paprika, plus extra to serve

65g (2¼oz) cooking chorizo, cut into small cubes

Flaky sea salt

Add the chickpeas to a food processor along with a little of their liquid and blitz until broken down. Add the tahini, the juice of ½ lemon, 1 garlic clove, olive oil, paprika and a good pinch of salt and blitz again until smooth. Taste to check the seasoning, adding more salt, lemon juice and garlic as needed. Blitz again, then taste to check the seasoning once more. If the hummus needs loosening, add an ice cube or a tablespoon of very cold water and blitz again, repeating until you reach your desired consistency.

Set a frying pan over a medium heat and add the cubed chorizo. Fry for 4–6 minutes until crispy and the fat has rendered out.

Spread the hummus over a plate, then spoon the crispy chorizo into the centre. Serve with an extra sprinkle of smoked paprika.

This is herby, creamy and filling. It's great served with more green veg – I love grilled broccoli here, but use raw carrots and cucumbers if keeping it fresher.

GREEN GODDESS

1 avocado, peeled and pitted

1 garlic clove, roughly chopped

1 shallot, roughly chopped

30g (1oz) baby spinach leaves

30g (1oz) basil leaves

80g (3oz) canned white beans, drained

1 tablespoon nutritional yeast

Juice of 1 lemon, or more to taste

2 tablespoons extra virgin olive oil

Flaky sea salt

Add all the ingredients with a generous pinch of salt to a high-speed blender and blitz until smooth, adding a splash of water if necessary. Taste, adding more salt or lemon juice as needed.

This dip is creamy from the beans, cheesy from the Parmesan and has an umami hit from the truffle oil. You can serve this with bread or vegetables, but you'll probably be happy eating it with a spoon.

TRUFFLE WHITE BEAN DIP

1 x 400g (14oz) can of cannellini beans, drained and liquid reserved

2 tablespoons truffle oil

Juice of ½ lemon

20g (¾oz) Parmesan, finely grated

Flaky sea salt and ground black pepper

Add the beans and some of their liquid to a food processor and blitz until broken down. Add the truffle oil, lemon juice, Parmesan and a good pinch each of salt and pepper and blitz again until smooth. Taste, adding more seasoning as needed. Serve with a few grinds of black pepper.

This is full of umami from the miso and sweetness from the caramelized onions. Serve with crunchy vegetables and use any leftovers to elevate your next sandwich.

MISO BUTTER BEAN DIP

1 onion, thinly sliced

3 tablespoons extra virgin olive oil

1 tablespoon white miso

200g (7oz) canned butter beans, plus a little of their liquid

Juice of ½–1 lemon, to taste

Flaky sea salt and ground black pepper

Add the sliced onion to a frying pan along with 2 tablespoons of the oil and a pinch of salt. Fry over a low-medium heat for 18–20 minutes, until softened and slightly caramelized. Add the miso and stir to combine, then remove from the heat.

Transfer the onions to a food processor along with the butter beans and a little of their liquid, the remaining tablespoon of oil and the juice of ½ lemon. Blitz until smooth, adding more of the bean liquid or some water to loosen if required. Taste, adding more lemon juice, salt and black pepper as desired.

Broad beans are so tasty and pack this dip with fibre. Serve this with grilled bread or tortilla chips.

BROAD BEAN DIP

250g (8¾oz) frozen or freshly podded broad beans

1 avocado, peeled and pitted

2 tablespoons extra virgin olive oil

10g (¼oz) dill, basil or mint leaves

Juice of 1 lemon

Flaky sea salt

Bring a pan of salted water to the boil, add the broad beans and simmer for 3–4 minutes. Drain, then plunge into a bowl of iced water to stop the cooking and preserve their nice green colour. Drain, then slip the beans out of their skins and add to a food processor.

Add the avocado, olive oil, dill, basil or mint and lemon juice to the food processor, with a generous pinch of salt. Blitz until smooth, adding more salt if needed.

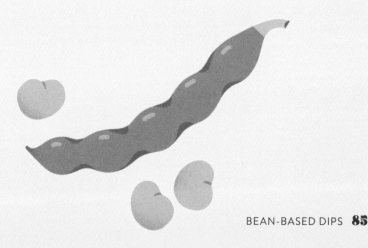

Blitzed black beans turn into a smoky, creamy dip that is delicious scooped up with crisps or crunchy vegetables. Use any leftovers to make breakfast tacos – load up with a fried egg, some cheese, coriander, jalapeños and hot sauce.

BLACK BEAN DIP

240g (8½oz) canned black beans, plus a little of their liquid

Juice of 1 lime

10g (¼oz) coriander leaves, plus extra to serve

2 teaspoons chipotle chilli paste

1 garlic clove, minced

Flaky sea salt

Feta or cotija cheese, to serve (optional)

Add the black beans and liquid, lime juice, coriander, chipotle paste, garlic and some salt to a food processor. Blitz until smooth, adding more salt if needed.

Serve with a few extra coriander leaves on top, and crumbled cheese, if using.

This dip has it all, with beans, guacamole, sour cream, salsa and cheese. You could make queso to serve alongside and use a couple of spoonfuls in place of the grated cheese. Serve when you're feeding a crowd and always buy more tortilla chips than you think you'll need!

LAYERED TACO DIP

1 tablespoon extra virgin olive oil

½ red onion, finely diced

240g (8½oz) canned black beans, plus a little of their liquid

1 tablespoon chipotle chilli paste

2 avocados, halved and pitted

1 fresh jalapeño or green chilli, finely diced

20g (¾oz) coriander, top of stalks and leaves finely chopped

Juice of 2 limes

2 large vine tomatoes, finely diced

150g (5oz) sour cream

60g (2¼oz) Cheddar, grated

30g (1oz) pickled jalapeños

Flaky sea salt

Add the olive oil to a frying pan and set over a medium heat. Tip in half the red onion and fry for 8–10 minutes until softened, then add the beans along with some of their liquid, and the chipotle paste. Cook for 5 minutes then remove from the heat and set aside to cool. Season to taste with salt.

Next, make the guacamole. Scoop the flesh from the avocados into a bowl and mash with a fork until broken down but still a little chunky. Add the jalapeño and half the coriander, then squeeze in the juice of 1 lime. Stir to combine and season to taste with salt.

Add the diced tomatoes to a bowl, along with the remaining red onion and coriander. Squeeze in the juice of the second lime and season generously with salt, then mix well.

To assemble, lay the black beans over the bottom of a dish and top with the guacamole. Spread the sour cream on top of that, then spoon over the salsa. Finish with the grated cheese and finally the pickled jalapeños and dig in.

VEGGIE HEROES DIPS

The key here is to make sure your avocados are ripe enough that they mash easily. This is how I like guacamole, but feel free to put your own spin on it – tomatoes are welcome to the party!

GUACAMOLE

3 ripe avocados

½ onion, finely chopped

1 fresh jalapeño, red or green chilli, finely chopped

15g (½oz) coriander, finely chopped

Juice of 1–2 limes, to taste

Flaky sea salt

Cut the avocados in half and remove the stones. Squeeze the flesh out from the skin and into a mixing bowl. Mash them with a fork until broken down but still chunky. Add the onion, chilli, coriander, juice of 1 lime and some salt and mash again to combine. Taste, adding more salt or lime juice if needed.

This salad-dip hybrid is seriously good scooped up on a salty tortilla chip. Based on the delicious Mexican street food esquites, this dip is sweet, salty and zingy.

MEXICAN STREET CORN DIP

2 tablespoons extra virgin olive oil

1 x 340g (12oz) can of sweetcorn, drained and patted dry

80g (3oz) sour cream

30g (1oz) mayonnaise

1 teaspoon chipotle chilli paste

100g (3½oz) feta, crumbled

10g (¼oz) coriander, roughly chopped

2 spring onions, thinly sliced

Juice of 1–2 limes, to taste

Flaky sea salt

Chilli flakes or powder, to serve (I like using ground chipotle chilli flakes)

Add the olive oil to a large frying pan and set over a medium-high heat. Once hot, add the sweetcorn and cook for 8–10 minutes until charred. Remove from the heat and set aside to cool slightly.

Once the sweetcorn has cooled, add it to a large mixing bowl along with the sour cream, mayonnaise, chipotle paste, feta, coriander, spring onions and the juice of 1 lime. Mix well to combine, then season with a little salt and more lime juice if desired. Serve with a sprinkle of chilli.

This is one of my favourite things to eat. A Middle-Eastern smoky aubergine dip that is very similar to baba ganoush, but creamier due to the addition of tahini. The flavour from the aubergines is unmatched, so make sure you really char the skin.

MUTABAL

2 medium aubergines

50g (2oz) tahini

1 garlic clove, minced

Juice of 1 lemon, or more to taste

2 tablespoons extra virgin olive oil, plus extra to serve

Small handful of parsley leaves, roughly chopped

Flaky sea salt

Pomegranate seeds, to serve

Pierce the aubergines all over with a fork. Char them over a flame for 10–15 minutes, turning often, until completely blackened and collapsing; you can do this under the grill if you don't have a gas hob. Transfer to a colander in the sink, cut into them lengthways and leave to cool and drain a bit.

Once cooled, peel away most of the charred skin and remove the stems. Add the aubergine flesh to a mixing bowl and use a fork to break it up. Add the tahini, garlic, lemon juice, olive oil, parsley and a pinch of salt, then mix well to combine. Taste, adding more salt or lemon juice if you like. Serve with an extra drizzle of olive oil and the pomegranate seeds scattered on top.

Originating in Catalonia, this comes together so quickly and is full of flavour. You could use fresh red peppers and char them over a flame – follow the same instructions for the aubergine in Mutabal on pages 96–97.

ROMESCO

300g (10½oz) roasted red peppers from a jar

100g (3½oz) sun-dried tomatoes, drained

100g (3½oz) blanched almonds, flaked almonds, hazelnuts or pine nuts, toasted

1 garlic clove, minced

1 tablespoon smoked paprika

2 tablespoons red wine vinegar or sherry vinegar, plus extra to taste

3 tablespoons extra virgin olive oil

Flaky sea salt

Add the peppers, tomatoes, nuts and garlic to a food processor or high-speed blender and blitz until broken down. Add the smoked paprika, vinegar and olive oil, along with a generous pinch of salt, and blitz again until smooth, adding a splash of water if needed. Taste to check the seasoning, adding more salt or vinegar if needed.

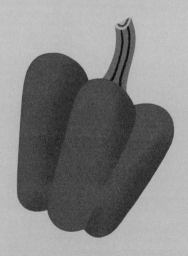

This is perfect for dipping summer rolls filled with lots of fresh herbs.

PEANUT DIPPING SAUCE

90g (3¼oz) peanut butter

2 tablespoons light soy sauce

2 tablespoons rice vinegar

1 tablespoon sesame oil

1 tablespoon honey

1 garlic clove, minced

Add all the ingredients to a bowl and whisk together. Add 1–2 tablespoons of water to loosen it slightly, until you have a smooth and creamy dip.

The key here is to use ripe, in-season tomatoes, so save this one for the summer months. You can chop the tomatoes as you like here, but I prefer them really broken down for easier dipping.

TOMATO SALSA

3 large vine-ripened tomatoes, very finely chopped

1 small red onion, finely chopped

1 fresh jalapeño, red or green chilli, finely chopped

Bunch of coriander, finely chopped

Juice of 2 limes, or more to taste

Flaky sea salt

In a bowl, combine the ingredients, with salt to taste, and toss well. Taste, adding more salt or lime juice if needed. Set aside to let the flavours come together before serving.

This Indian-inpired chutney uses fresh ingredients and requires no cooking, different to cooked, relish-like chutneys. I like the addition of yoghurt to make a thicker dip.

CORIANDER CHUTNEY DIP

30g (1oz) coriander

15g (½oz) mint, leaves removed

Juice of ½–1 lemon, to taste

2 tablespoons extra virgin olive oil

150g (5oz) thick Greek yoghurt

Flaky sea salt

Add the coriander, mint leaves, the juice of ½ lemon and the olive oil to a blender, along with a splash of water. Blitz until completely smooth, then stir through the yoghurt and season to taste with salt, adding more lemon juice if needed.

Sweet, spicy and zingy, this salsa is a great alternative to switch things up from a classic tomato salsa. Serve with tortilla chips and have any leftovers with grilled meat or fish.

CHARRED PINEAPPLE SALSA

250g (9oz) peeled fresh pineapple, cut into chunky slices

1 red chilli

1 small red onion, finely diced

20g (¾oz) coriander, top of stalks and leaves finely chopped

100g (3½oz) roasted red peppers from a jar, finely chopped

Juice of 1 lime

Flaky sea salt

Set a frying pan over a high heat. Once hot, add the pineapple and whole chilli and char for 6–8 minutes, turning often to make sure every side gets some colour. Remove from the heat and set aside to cool.

Once cooled, finely chop the pineapple and transfer to a large bowl. Scrape away most of the burnt skin from the chilli, then finely chop and put that in the bowl, too. Add the red onion, coriander, red peppers and lime juice and toss to combine. Season to taste with salt and serve.

This takes five minutes to make and is so full of flavour. I like to serve it with goats' cheese or ricotta, plus crostini to spread a little tapenade and cheese onto for a perfect bite.

OLIVE TAPENADE

200g (7oz) pitted Kalamata olives

50g (2oz) sun-dried tomatoes

1 tablespoon capers

4 tablespoons extra virgin olive oil

1 garlic clove, roughly chopped

Small handful of basil leaves

Add all the ingredients to a food processor and blitz until everything is well chopped, but not smooth – you want to retain some texture.

This is my take on the Levantine dish muhammara, a smoky dip made from red peppers, walnuts, olive oil, and often bread.

ROASTED RED PEPPER AND WALNUT DIP

90g (3¼oz) walnuts

300g (10½oz) roasted red peppers from a jar

50g (2oz) fresh breadcrumbs

2 tablespoons extra virgin olive oil, plus extra to serve

1 teaspoon ground cumin

2 teaspoons Aleppo chilli flakes (pul biber)

1 tablespoon tomato paste

2 tablespoons pomegranate molasses

Juice of ½–1 lemon, to taste

Flaky sea salt

Add 80g (3oz) of the walnuts, the red peppers, breadcrumbs, olive oil, cumin, chilli flakes, tomato paste, pomegranate molasses, juice of ½ lemon and some salt to a food processor. Blitz until broken down to your desired consistency. Taste, adding more salt or lemon juice as needed.

Serve with the remaining walnuts broken over the top, and drizzled generously with olive oil.

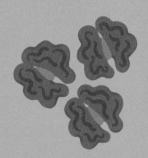

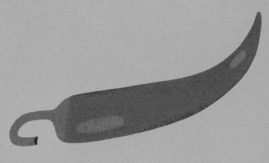

This dip is one of my absolute favourites.
The flavour from the burnt spring onions is
unmatched and you can adjust the wasabi to
make it as punchy as you like. A lot of the dips
in this book would be good with fries dunked
into them, but this might be the best.

BURNT SPRING ONION AND WASABI MAYO

6 spring onions, ends trimmed

1 fat garlic clove, peeled

Thumb-sized piece of ginger, peeled and roughly chopped

1 tablespoon vegetable oil

2 teaspoons wasabi, plus more to taste

100g (3½oz) sour cream

30g (1oz) mayonnaise

1 teaspoon rice wine vinegar

Flaky sea salt

Set a frying pan over a very high heat and add the spring onions. Cook for 6–8 minutes, turning often, until very charred, adding the garlic to the pan for the final minute and turning it once to char on both sides.

Add the spring onions and garlic to a food processor along with the ginger, vegetable oil and 1 teaspoon of wasabi. Blitz until broken down and well chopped.

Add the sour cream, mayonnaise and vinegar to a bowl and mix well to combine, then stir through the spring onion mixture. Taste, adding salt and extra wasabi as/if needed.

This is a dip based on the Greek dish skordalia, comprising a combination of garlic with potatoes, nuts and stale bread, lots of olive oil and some vinegar.

GREEK GARLIC AND POTATO DIP

450g (1lb) Maris Piper potatoes, peeled and cut into even chunks

80g (3oz) blanched almonds

4 garlic cloves, roughly chopped

2 tablespoons red wine vinegar

100ml (3½fl oz) extra virgin olive oil

1 spring onion, thinly sliced

Flaky sea salt

Add the potatoes to a medium saucepan and cover with cold water. Add some salt, then set over a medium heat and bring to the boil. Once boiling, reduce to a simmer and cook for 15 minutes or until the potatoes can be easily pierced with a fork.

In the meantime, add the almonds, garlic and vinegar to a food processor and blitz until broken down and the consistency of a paste, adding a little water if needed.

Drain the potatoes and, while still warm, mash them as much as you can. Add the almond paste and stir to combine, then gradually add the olive oil, mixing well between each addition to incorporate. If it is too thick, add some water to loosen. Season to taste with salt and serve at room temperature, topped with the spring onions.

I really, really love this dip. It's sweet and salty, and the nutty browned butter is just so delicious. Be sure to do the browned butter just before serving so it is warm and melted.

MAPLE SWEET POTATO DIP WITH BACON

850g (2lb) sweet potatoes, peeled and cut into 2cm (¾in) chunks

4 tablespoons extra virgin olive oil

3 tablespoons maple syrup

1 teaspoon cinnamon

1 teaspoon smoked paprika

4 rashers streaky bacon

15g (½oz) unsalted butter

30g (1oz) pecans, roughly chopped

Flaky sea salt

Preheat the oven to 200°C/180°C fan (400°F) Gas 6. On a large roasting tray, toss the chopped sweet potato in 2 tablespoons of olive oil, 2 tablespoons of maple syrup, the spices and a generous pinch of salt. Transfer to the oven for 40–50 minutes until soft, tossing halfway through. Remove from the oven and set aside to cool.

Add a tablespoon of olive oil to a frying pan and set over a medium heat. Add the bacon and fry on both sides until crispy, then remove onto kitchen paper to drain any excess fat and cool down. Add the cooked sweet potato and remaining tablespoon of olive oil to a food processor and blitz until completely smooth. Taste, adding a little more salt if needed.

Add the butter to the same pan you cooked the bacon in and set over a medium heat. Once melted, add the pecans and cook for 2–3 minutes, until the butter is browned and smells nutty. Remove from the heat and stir in the remaining tablespoon of maple syrup.

Swirl the sweet potato dip onto a serving dish. Spoon over the butter and pecans, then crumble over the crispy bacon to finish.

This is sweet, smoky and very easy to make. It's packed with goodness from the carrots and the beans and is a real crowd-pleaser. Serve with toasted pitta bread, tortilla chips or raw vegetables.

ROASTED CARROT DIP

550g (1lb 4½oz) carrots, peeled and cut into 1cm (½in) rounds

2 tablespoons extra virgin olive oil

100g (3½oz) canned white beans, plus 2 tablespoons of their liquid

1 teaspoon smoked paprika

Juice of ½–1 lemon, to taste

Flaky sea salt

Preheat the oven to 200°C/180°C fan (400°F) Gas 6.

Toss the carrots with the olive oil and place in a roasting tray in a single layer. Sprinkle generously with salt and transfer to the oven to bake for 1 hour, turning halfway through. Remove from the oven and leave to cool.

Add the cooled carrots to a food processor along with the beans, smoked paprika and the juice of ½ lemon. Blitz until well broken down, then add the bean liquid and blitz again until smooth. Taste, adding more salt or lemon juice if needed.

The Italian dish panzanella is one of my favourite things to eat when tomatoes are at their best. Serve with grilled bread like the traditional dish, or with crisps or tortilla chips if you prefer. Sub in whatever ripe fruit you have – I often reach for strawberries or melon here.

PANZANELLA-INSPIRED SALSA

2 large tomatoes (beef, heirloom or something similar), finely diced

1 roasted red pepper from a jar, finely diced

⅓ cucumber, finely diced

1 nectarine or peach, pitted and finely diced

½ red onion, finely diced

1 tablespoon capers, finely chopped

Handful of basil leaves, torn

2 tablespoons extra virgin olive oil

1 tablespoon red wine vinegar

1 garlic clove, minced

Flaky sea salt and ground black pepper

Add the tomatoes, red pepper, cucumber, nectarine or peach, red onion, capers and basil to a bowl and mix well to combine, seasoning generously with salt and pepper. In a small bowl, whisk the olive oil, vinegar and garlic together, then pour over the salsa. Mix well then cover and leave to sit at room temperature for at least 20 minutes before topping with the basil and serving with grilled bread.

MEAT AND FISH DIPS

I made this with Kalamata olives once and have never gone back. It is so flavoursome yet so quick to make. While this northern Italian sauce is traditionally served with veal, I serve this dip with grilled bread, roasted vegetables or crudités.

OLIVE TONNATO

100g (3½oz) jarred or canned tuna

1 egg yolk

½ garlic clove

2 anchovy fillets in oil

25g (1oz) pitted Kalamata olives

1 teaspoon Dijon mustard

Juice of ½–1 lemon, to taste

120ml (4fl oz) extra virgin olive oil

Flaky sea salt and ground black pepper

Add the tuna, egg yolk, garlic, anchovies, olives and mustard to a food processor with the juice of ½ lemon and blitz to a paste. With the motor still running, start to add the olive oil very slowly. Once all of the oil is added and you have a sauce the consistency of a loose mayonnaise, season to taste with salt and pepper, adding more lemon juice if desired.

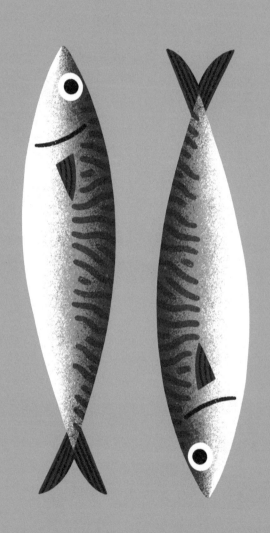

This is my mum's recipe and it is a real winner – full of flavour while still being light, and it only takes five minutes to make. She serves it with oatcakes or melba toast and celery, but you can dip any crunchy vegetables, crackers or bread here.

SMOKED MACKEREL AND WHIPPED RICOTTA

200g (7oz) smoked mackerel, skin removed

250g (9oz) ricotta

1–2 teaspoons horseradish sauce, plus more to taste

Juice of ½–1 lemon

Flaky sea salt and ground black pepper

10g (¼oz) chives, finely chopped, to garnish

Add the smoked mackerel, ricotta, horseradish and the juice of ½ lemon to a food processor and blitz until relatively smooth but retaining some texture. Season to taste with salt and pepper, adding more lemon juice and horseradish as desired.

Serve garnished with the chives.

This dip is great eaten with cucumber and nori sheets. You can put your own spin on it by using finely diced salmon or tuna; just make sure to buy sushi-grade fish.

CRAB AND AVOCADO DIP

200g (7oz) white crab meat

10g (¼oz) chives, finely chopped

30g (1oz) mayonnaise

30g (1oz) thick Greek yoghurt

½ teaspoon sriracha, plus more to taste

Juice of 1 lime

1 avocado, peeled, pitted and finely diced

2 tablespoons toasted sesame seeds

Flaky sea salt

In a bowl, mix the crab meat, chives, mayonnaise, yoghurt, sriracha and half of the lime juice together until well combined. Season to taste with salt, plus more sriracha or lime juice as desired.

Transfer the crab mixture to a serving dish then cover the top with the diced avocado. Sprinkle over the sesame seeds to serve.

This is a great one to serve at a party. Get it ready ahead of time, then slide it into the oven and wow your guests with a bubbling dish of pure comfort food. Serve with thick-cut crisps – this one's a little weightier!

BUFFALO CHICKEN DIP

165g (5¾oz) cream cheese

75g (2½oz) sour cream

5 tablespoons hot sauce (I like Valentina)

200g (7oz) grated mozzarella

4 spring onions, thinly sliced

300g (10½oz) cooked chicken, shredded

Preheat the oven to 200°C/180°C fan (400°F) Gas 6.

In a large mixing bowl, stir together the cream cheese, sour cream, hot sauce and three-quarters of the mozzarella. Once well combined, add the spring onions and chicken and mix again. Transfer to an ovenproof dish, then sprinkle over the remaining mozzarella. Cook in the oven for 20–25 minutes until bubbling and the cheese is golden. Leave to stand for 5–10 minutes before digging in.

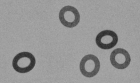

I wanted to make a dip that was an ode to fried olives. This is what I came up with, and I really love it. The crispy sausage and creamy ricotta is a great combination. This one really should be served with bread, ensuring you can get some ricotta, sausage and olive in one bite.

RICOTTA, OLIVE AND CRISPY SAUSAGE DIP

2 tablespoons extra virgin olive oil, plus extra to serve

2 good-quality Italian sausages, casings removed

70g (2½oz) large green olives, pitted and roughly chopped

½ teaspoon chilli flakes

250g (9oz) ricotta

20g (¾oz) Parmesan, finely grated

Grated zest and juice of 1 lemon

Flaky sea salt and ground black pepper

Set a frying pan over a medium-high heat and add the olive oil. Once hot, add the sausages and break them up into small pieces with a wooden spoon. Fry for 8–10 minutes until browned and crispy, then tip into a bowl. Add the olives and chilli flakes and mix together.

In a separate bowl, mix the ricotta, Parmesan, half of the lemon zest and juice until smooth. Season to taste with salt and pepper, adding more lemon zest and juice if desired.

Serve the ricotta mixture spread over a plate with the sausage and olive mix piled into the middle.

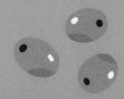

Inspired by the Mexican dish frijoles puercos, this dip is smoky and a little spicy. Add some cheese if you want – either melt some Cheddar into the mix, or serve with feta or cotija crumbled over the top.

CHORIZO BEAN DIP

200g (7oz) canned pinto or black beans, their liquid reserved

30g (1oz) pickled jalapeños

½ tablespoon chipotle chilli paste

75g (2½oz) chorizo, finely diced

1 garlic clove, minced

Add the beans to a food processor, along with the jalapeños and chipotle paste. Blitz until smooth, adding enough of their reserved liquid a little at a time to help the mixture break down and turn into a thick, creamy dip.

Add the chorizo to a frying pan and set over a medium heat. Cook for 2–3 minutes until crispy and the fat has rendered, then add the garlic and cook for a minute longer.

Add the bean mixture to the pan and stir to combine, cooking for a final 2 minutes. Serve hot.

This dip is inspired by the sloppy Joe sandwich – it's hearty, cheesy and a great one to have on the table when feeding a crowd. Serve with garlic bread or some sturdy crisps!

SLOPPY JOE DIP

1 tablespoon extra virgin olive oil

1 onion, finely chopped

1 garlic clove, minced

1 fresh green chilli, finely chopped

250g (9oz) minced beef

300ml (10½fl oz) passata

2 tablespoons tomato ketchup

1 tablespoon brown sugar

A few good splashes of Worcestershire sauce

75g (2½oz) Cheddar or mozzarella, grated

Flaky sea salt and ground black pepper

Heat the olive oil in an ovenproof frying pan over a medium heat. Add the onion and a pinch of salt and cook for 10 minutes until softened, then add the garlic and chilli and cook for 2 minutes longer. Add the beef to the pan and cook for 6–8 minutes until browned, breaking any large clumps up with a wooden spoon.

Add the passata, ketchup, sugar and Worcestershire sauce and mix well to combine. Simmer for 8–10 minutes until slightly thickened. Season to taste with salt and pepper, adding more Worcestershire sauce if you like.

Heat the grill to medium-high. Sprinkle the cheese over the top of the mixture in the pan, then place under the grill for 2–3 minutes until the cheese is melted and golden.

Serve this with fresh garlic bread for a real crowd-pleaser. Feel free to switch out the pepperoni for your favourite pizza topping.

PIZZA DIP

450g (1lb) cherry tomatoes, quartered

1 tablespoon olive oil

1 garlic clove, minced

Small bunch of basil, leaves only, plus extra to serve

200g (7oz) cream cheese

100g (3½oz) mozzarella

50g (2oz) pepperoni (optional)

Flaky sea salt and ground black pepper

Preheat the oven to 200°C/180°C fan (400°F) Gas 6.

Add the tomatoes and olive oil to an ovenproof frying pan and set over a medium-high heat. Cook for 8–10 minutes, squashing the tomatoes with the back of a wooden spoon until jammy. Add the garlic and basil and cook for 2 minutes more, then remove from the heat.

Combine the cream cheese and mozzarella with some salt and pepper in a small bowl. Spread over the top of the tomatoes, then arrange the pepperoni, if using, on top. Transfer to the oven to bake for 15–20 minutes, until golden and bubbling, then remove and leave to stand for 5 minutes. Serve with basil leaves scattered on top.

SWEET DIPS

This dip is based on a blueberry cheesecake. For that reason, I'd recommend serving with digestive biscuits or graham crackers for the full effect!

BLUEBERRY CREAM CHEESE

120g (4oz) blueberries

200g (7oz) cream cheese

50g (2oz) icing sugar

50g (2oz) thick Greek yoghurt

1 teaspoon vanilla bean paste

Add the blueberries to a bowl and use a fork to mash them a little so they release some of their juices.

In a separate bowl, use a balloon whisk to whisk the cream cheese until creamy, then sift in the icing sugar and whisk again until smooth. Add the yoghurt and vanilla and stir to combine.

Finally, add the blueberries and stir a final three or four times until they are rippled throughout the cream cheese mixture.

This dip couldn't be easier. Honey, yoghurt, delicious peaches and thyme. Serve with biscuits to dip – buttery shortbread or an oaty biscuit are my favourites here.

FROZEN PEACH WITH WHIPPED HONEY YOGHURT AND THYME

200g (7oz) thick Greek yoghurt

150g (5oz) double cream

2 tablespoons honey, plus extra to serve

1 frozen peach or nectarine

20g (¾oz) toasted flaked almonds

2 sprigs of thyme

Place your peach or nectarine in the freezer for at least 12 hours or overnight to freeze fully.

Add the yoghurt, cream and honey to a bowl and whip to soft peaks. Spoon into a serving dish and grate the frozen peach or nectarine all over. Sprinkle over the toasted almonds and thyme leaves, then serve with an extra drizzle of honey.

I love banoffee pie and it's just as good in dip form. Serve with ginger nuts, Lotus biscuits or digestives to dunk.

BANOFFEE DIP

2 bananas

150g (5oz) salted caramel or dulce de leche

400ml (13½fl oz) double cream

1 teaspoon vanilla bean paste

10g (¼oz) dark chocolate, to finish

Peel and add 1 of the bananas to a bowl and mash well with a fork, then stir through the salted caramel or dulce de leche until well combined. Slice the remaining banana into rounds.

Add the cream to a large bowl with the vanilla and whip to soft peaks.

To assemble, first spoon the banana caramel on to the bottom of your serving dish, then lay the sliced banana over the top. Spoon over the whipped cream and finish by grating the chocolate on top.

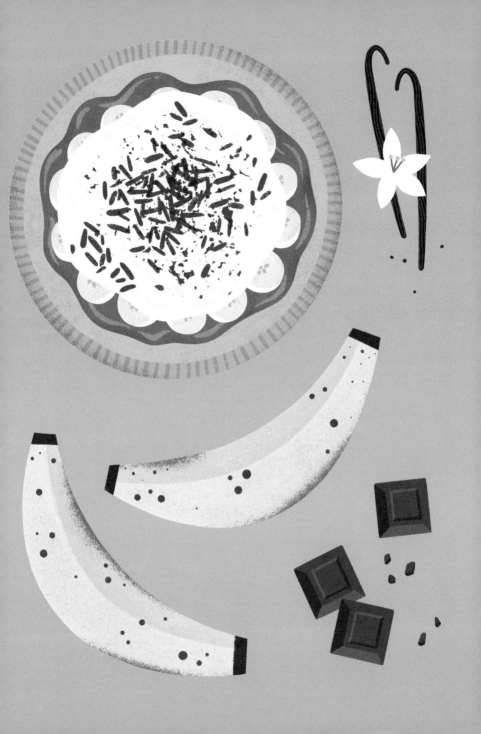

A sweet and salty dip that'll get you practising your caramel-making techniques. This recipe makes a direct caramel first – take your time and don't stir until there's a good amount of caramel in there already. Dip fresh fruit, churros or mini donuts in this one.

SALTED CARAMEL

240g (8½oz) caster sugar

100g (3½oz) unsalted butter

150ml (5fl oz) double cream

Good pinch of flaky sea salt

Set a sauté pan over a medium-low heat and add 3 tablespoons of the sugar. Cook undisturbed until the sugar melts and turns a light golden colour, then sprinkle in 3 or 4 tablespoons more. Again, cook until the sugar melts, tilting the pan slightly to distribute. Repeat this process 3 or 4 more times, using a spatula at this stage to stir the caramel between additions.

Once all the sugar has melted and is an amber colour, add in the butter and allow to melt before pouring in the cream. Whisk together and allow to bubble for 1 minute before adding the salt and setting aside to cool.

This caramel sauce is made with just three ingredients, requires no cooking and yet does not compromise on flavour. I like the addition of miso for an umami hit, but feel free to omit and keep it classic with just vanilla. Serve with fresh fruit – I think apples and pears are great here.

MISO DATE CARAMEL

200g (7oz) Medjool dates, pitted

1 tablespoon white miso

1 teaspoon vanilla extract

Soak the dates in just-boiled water for 10 minutes to soften, then drain completely. Transfer them to a food processor and blitz until broken down. With the motor still running, slowly stream in water until you reach your desired consistency and have a thick, smooth sauce.

Add the miso and vanilla then blitz again to combine.

This is the kind of chocolate sauce you'd serve with churros. Serve in mugs so you can dip and sip at the same time!

CHOCOLATE SAUCE

200ml (7fl oz) whole milk

1 tablespoon caster sugar

100g (3½oz) dark chocolate, about 70%, chopped

1 teaspoon vanilla extract

100ml (3½fl oz) double cream

Pinch of flaky sea salt

Churros, to serve

Add the milk and sugar to a small saucepan and set over a medium-low heat. Heat until the milk is steaming, then add the chocolate. Allow the chocolate to melt for a minute, then whisk until smooth. Add the vanilla and simmer gently for about 5 minutes until thickened.

Remove from the heat and pour in the cream, then finish with the salt. Serve alongside your churros and tuck in.

This is a perfect low-effort yet still chic pudding to serve at your next dinner party. You'll be away from the table for just five minutes and return with a bowl of glossy chocolate fondue ready for dipping. Keep it classic and serve with strawberries to dip.

CHOCOLATE FONDUE

100g (3½oz) milk chocolate, finely chopped

100g (3½oz) dark chocolate, finely chopped

100ml (3½fl oz) double cream

50ml (2fl oz) whole milk

Flaky sea salt

Add both the chocolates to a saucepan along with the cream and set over a low-medium heat. Heat gently until the chocolate has all melted, then add the milk and mix well until smooth and glossy. Season to taste with salt and serve immediately.

This dip is really amazing! You'd never know that it has tofu in it, so you can enjoy a rich, chocolatey pud AND fill up on protein. Serve with fresh fruit, or if you like sweet and salty together, definitely try this with some salted crisps.

VEGAN CHOCOLATE DIP

200g (7oz) dark chocolate, at least 70%, finely chopped

300g (10½oz) silken tofu, drained

1–2 tablespoons maple syrup

Flaky sea salt

Add the chocolate to a heatproof bowl and set over a pan of gently simmering water, making sure the base of the bowl isn't touching the water. Leave until the chocolate has melted, stirring every so often, then set aside to cool.

Add the drained tofu to a food processor and pour in the cooled, melted chocolate. Blitz until smooth and well combined, then add a tablespoon of maple syrup and a good pinch of salt. Blitz again, then taste and add more maple syrup if it isn't sweet enough. Serve sprinkled with extra flaky salt.

This dip requires next to no effort and is ready to eat in less than five minutes. Be careful not to burn the marshmallows; they'll toast much more quickly under the grill than over a fire!

S'MORES

200g (7oz) milk or dark chocolate, broken into pieces

100g (3½oz) marshmallows, cut in half

Digestive biscuits or graham crackers to dip

Set the grill to medium-high. Spread the chocolate over the base of an ovenproof dish and top with the halved marshmallows. Transfer to the grill and cook for 1–2 minutes, keeping a close eye so the marshmallows don't burn. Remove from the grill and get dunking!

This has all the best bits of a tiramisu –
the creamy mascarpone mix, coffee flavour
and plenty of cocoa. Dip fresh strawberries
or madeleines in this one, for more of a
tiramisu vibe.

TIRAMISU DIP

180ml (6fl oz) double cream

60g (2¼oz) dark chocolate, about 70%, finely chopped

½ teaspoon instant coffee granules

Pinch of flaky sea salt

100g (3½oz) mascarpone

1 tablespoon coffee liqueur (I like Kahlúa)

Unsweetened cocoa powder, to finish

Add 80ml (2¾fl oz) of the cream to a small saucepan
and heat until steaming. Remove from the heat, add
the chocolate, instant coffee and salt. Leave for
a minute, then whisk until smooth and glossy.
Set aside to cool.

In a bowl, whip the remaining cream to soft peaks.
In a separate bowl, mix the mascarpone and coffee
liqueur until combined. Use a spoon to gently fold
the whipped cream into the mascarpone mix.

To assemble, spoon half the chocolate ganache
over the base of a shallow bowl. Top with half
the mascarpone cream, then repeat once more.
Dust with cocoa powder before serving.

Achieve the flavours of a cinnamon roll in five minutes and without having to turn the oven on. Serve with fresh fruit or brioche.

CINNAMON ROLL DIP

200g (7oz) cream cheese

100g (3½oz) icing sugar

100g (3½oz) thick Greek yoghurt

30g (1oz) butter, melted

30g (1oz) brown sugar

2 teaspoons ground cinnamon

Add the cream cheese to a large bowl and use a balloon whisk to whisk until smooth and creamy. Sift in the icing sugar and whisk again until smooth and fully incorporated. Add the yoghurt and mix again.

In a separate bowl, mix the melted butter, brown sugar and cinnamon until smooth.

Add the cinnamon butter to the cream cheese in stages, gently folding to create a ripple throughout.

UK/US GLOSSARY

Aubergine – eggplant

Beetroot – beet

Biscuits – cookies

Broad beans – fava beans

Caster sugar – superfine sugar

Chicory – endive

Coriander – cilantro

Courgette – zucchini

Crisps – potato chips

Digestive biscuits – graham crackers

Double cream – heavy cream

Flaked almonds – slivered almonds

Ginger nuts – ginger snaps

Grill – broiler

Icing sugar – confectioners' sugar

Minced beef – ground beef

Passata – strained tomatoes

Pepper – bell pepper

Prawns – shrimp

Sieve – strainer

Spring onions – scallions

Sultanas – golden raisins

INDEX